Love Letter To The Blue Planet

Elaine V. Emans

Pocahontas Press, Inc.
Blacksburg, Virginia

Love Letter to the Blue Planet by Elaine V. Emans
©1991 by Pocahontas Press, Inc.

Published by Pocahontas Press, Inc., Blacksburg, Virginia U.S.A.
Typesetting and Printing by Commonwealth Press,
   Radford, Virginia, U.S.A.

All rights reserved. No part of this book may be reproduced in any form or by any electronic or mechanical means including information storage and retrieval systems without permission in writing from the publisher, except by a reviewer who may quote brief passages in a review.

ISBN 0-936015-29-2
First Printing 1991

Library of Congress Cataloging in Publication Data:

Emans, Elaine V. 1911 —
   Love Letter to the Blue Planet/Elaine V. Emans.
       p.   cm.
   ISBN 0-936015-29-2 : $5.95
   I. Title.
   PS3555.M28L68   1991
   811'.54—dc20   91-31755
                                                               CIP

Love Letter To The Blue Planet

Acknowledgments	vi
Dear Earth	3
1 — Question without Answer	4
Jacques-Yves Cousteau	5
The Sun	6
For Rainer Maria Rilke on his "Sonnets to Orpheus"	7
The Undreamed	8
Exhortation	9
Obit Reread	10
Albrecht Durer	11
Thoreau Calls on Whitman	12
Coleridge, Praise	13
Wilde in the Highest City in the United States, 1882	14
Standing up the Sweet Corn	15
For "Madame Cezanne in the Conservatory"	16
What Bird?	17
2 — The Game Players	18
Villanelle for Prairie Dogs	19
Missing Red Squirrel	20
For a Lady Naming a Chipmunk "Ethelred the Unready"	21
Night Mission	22
The Hosing Down	23
Cat Fight, 5 a.m.	24
The Cats of Colette	25
The White Cat	26
Interview with Rover's Ghost	27
Reply to an Inquiry as to Why I Haven't Answered a Letter	28
Last Night I Dreamed	29
The Prophet	30

3 — Bone to Pick with Silken Creatures 31
For a Mexican Spiny Pocket Mouse 32
Mouse in the Morning 33
Horseshoe Crabs 34
A Snake in the Hands 35
The Frog 36
Rotifer, Rotifer 37

4 — Draw at the Zoo 38
Take-over at the Symphony 39
Puffins 40
Filling the Suet Basket 41
"Crows in the Wheat Fields" 42
Macaw at the Zoo 43
Courtship Dance of the Common House Sparrow 44
May Morning at the Game Farm 45

5 — Talking to the Swans 46
Bow Tie 47
Tardy Thanksgiving 48
Cycles 49
Request 50
Moot Point 51

6 — Poem to the Brain 52
Song for Red Blood Cells 53
On Discovering that One of My Three
    Brains is Reptilian 54
Talking to My Cells 55
Oh, to Wear the Bones of a Bird Inside 56

7 — Post Card from Norway 57
A Matter of Nomenclature 58
At the Concert 59

8 — Old Photo of a Young Teacher 60
Mother as Student of Physiology 61
Amaryllis Unfolding 62
Father and the Blue Shirt 63
Father Recalled as Dinner Companion 64
Peonies 65

9 — The Lost Worm 66
Error 67
Mourning Cloak 68
Ant, Grooming 69

10 — Pteranodon 70
Seismosaurus 71
Newcomer 72

11 — Scenes from an Exercise 73
Waiting for Venus 74
On Finding a Child's Dump Truck
   on the Road to the Dump 75
Elegy 76
Self-Service 77
People Are Getting into Plants These Days 79
Timberdoodle 80
Incident at Camp 81
Snow-Cave 82
Muse Away 83
Note to be Taped to a Door-Knocker 84

Acknowledgments

Grateful acknowledgment is made to the following publications, which first printed some of the poems in this book:

America
"Pteranodon" — December 1985
"Scenes from an Exercise" — October 1986

Ball State University Forum
(which holds the international copyright)
"The Last Trip" — Summer 1974
"Obit Reread" — about 1976

Bluegrass Literary Review
"For Madame Cezanne in the Conservatory" — Fall 1981

Blue Unicorn
"Elegy" — June 1984
"For Miss Martha Who Knew Sir Walter Scott" — June 1988
"Standing Up the Sweet Corn" — June 1987

The Cape Rock
"Takeover at the Symphony" — 1979
"Cycles" — Winter 1983
"The Snow Cave" — Spring 1985

Centennial Review
"Peonies" — Summer 1985
"Coleridge, Praise" — Fall 1987

Colorado-North Review
"On Discovering that One of My Three Brains is Reptilian" — Spring 1980

Christian Science Monitor
"Macaw at the Zoo" — October 10, 1986
"Albrecht Durer" — October 26, 1988

Epos
"For Rainer Maria Rilke" — No. 3, 1976
"Rotifer" — No. 3, 1976

Four Quarters
"Father Recalled as Dinner Companion" — June 1980

Kansas Quarterly
"The Undreamed" — Winter 1980
"Mother As Student of Physiology" — Winter 1980
"Wilde in the Highest City in the U.S." — Winter/Spring 1988
"The Frog" — Summer 1988
"Muse Away" — Volume 22, number 8
Laurel Review
"Bow Tie" — 1983
Literary Review
"Interview with Rover's Ghost" — Summer 1987
The Lyric
"Post Card from Norway" — Summer 1966
"Request" — Spring 1968
"Missing Red Squirrel" — Winter 1969
"Tardy Thanksgiving" — Winter 1971
"For A Lady Naming a Chipmunk Ethelred the Unready — Winter 1979
"The White Cat" — Winter 1988
Michigan Quarterly Review
"Villanelle for Prairie Dogs" — Spring 1980
"Night Mission" — 1985
Midwest Quarterly — "On Finding a Child's Dump Truck" — Autumn 1975
Mikrokosmos
"A Matter of Nomenclature" — Fall 1976
Mississippi Valley Review
"Mourning cloak" — Fall/Winter 1981
"Filling the Suet-Basket" — about 1988
Lake Superior Review
"Talking to the Swans" — Winter 1978
Orphic Lute
"Cat Fight" — Fall 1988
"Amaryllis Unfolding" — Fall/Winter 1989
"Bone to Pick with Silken Creatures" — Summer 1989
Piedmont Literary Review
"Moot Point" — Spring/Summer 1985

Pikestaff Review
"Talking to My Cells" — about 1980
Plains Poetry Journal
"Horseshoe Crabs" — October 1983
Poet Lore
"Exhortation" — 1969-72
"Mouse in the Morning" — 1969-72
"A Snake in the Hands" — 1969-72
Prairie Schooner
"Error" — 1968 (reprinted by permission of the University of Nebraska Press)
Serpentine
"Last Night I Dreamed" — 1983
Song
"For Brueghel the Elder" — Fall/Winter 1982
Spoon River Quarterly
"Crows in the Wheat Fields" — Spring 1980
SPSM&H, Amelia
"At the Concert"
Texas Review
"Song for Red Blood Cells" — Spring 1981
"Oh, to Wear the Bones of a Bird" — Winter 1985
"Honey Bee" — No. 1/2, 1987
"What Bird" — No. 1/2, 1987
Virginia Quarterly Review
"The Game-Players" — Summer 1971
"The Hosing Down" — Summer 1971
"Ant, Grooming" — Summer 1971
Welter
"Father and the Blue Shirt" — 1985
Wind
"Puffins" — Volume 17, 1987
"People Are Getting into Plants" — Volume 17, 1987
Yankee
"Lost Worm" — August 1981

To the Cherished Memory of Billy

Dear Earth,

    There is little need for you to set
your cap this jauntily to win me: you
who would require twenty life-times, and yet
more, to be adequately admired, Blue
water Planet, spinning...
    Were you less
exquisitely fashioned in minutiae,
less heaped with mountain ranges so impressive,
with fewer interjacent glories, from your wee
wood mice, gaudy macaws, to reticulated
pythons and giraffes, inevitably you would
possess my heart as now.
    Had He created
you differently, Earth, you had been good
to cherish, too!
    In every particular
of your imperiled, terrestrial Self, you are
        my true love.

Elaine V. Emans

P.S. What a singular honor when *Time Magazine*
called you Person of the Year!

1

Question Without Answer

> *"Is the Universe Friendly?"*
> Albert Einstein

You didn't ask your question in the manner
in which we say, Is that dog friendly, growling
and wagging its tail? Does the Activist's new
                                banner
seem convincing? Is a certain country spoiling
for skirmishes with us? Are laughter and mirth
the healers they are claimed to be? Is cold
Antarctica the last of unspoiled earth?
Do young hearts fly in the face of growing old?

Oh, no. Your question, sir, is the essential
one facing all of us, and, answered *yes*
to, leads us to half-believing consequential
good awaits our finding it to cheer and bless.

Yes to your question hints at the arrival
of earth's regeneration, our survival.

Jacques-Yves Cousteau,

you call Earth the Water Planet
and rightly so.

I, loving color, call it the Blue
Planet as adoringly as you
say Water.

Yet both of us deplore
in the same word and breath
disastrous despoiling of the Sea
and our island Earth.

The Sun

> *"Is it so small a thing*
> *To have enjoyed the sun,*
> *To have lived light in the Spring?"*
> Matthew Arnold

How refreshing to hear your query
who knew the shadows of "Requiscat,"
the gloom of "The Forsaken Merman,"
the mourning in "Thyrsis" for your dead friend,
                        Arthur Clough,
and the deep melancholy of "Dover
                           Beach."

How good to know, Sir,
that for you light over-
came the pall of darkness —
and Sun at Spring's footfall
reached to your innermost cell.

For Rainer Maria Rilke on His "Sonnets to Orpheus"

You supposed the reason animals
were so full of silence when Orpheus
                            was singing
was that they were listening —
deep in temples within their ears?

Even between roarings, squeakings,
howlings, mewings, bellowings,
pipings, gruntings, bleatings,
screamings, moaning, crying, laughing
animals are always listening, Sir.

The Undreamed

> *"Some species are necessary as prey
> and others as predators...
> One cannot rationally conceive
> a state of things where there
> were flies without swallows,
> and vice versa."*
> Cuvier

We have states of things you never
                dreamed of, Sir:
flies without swallows dipping,
                scooping them with tiny
bills open, ringed with sticky bristles;
                twilight without
twitterings and grace to trap the heart.

We have fish without bald eagles, deer
                without wolves.
We soon may have Dutch-elm beetles
                without elms —
only hopefully vice versa.

Nor was your vision long enough to see US,
                predators,
                with disappearing prey.

Exhortation

*On learning that a proposed major
International Airport, to be built next
to a Wildlife Area, had been voted down.*

Praise the Lord and the referral committee —
Your wilderness is saved, saved!
Praise them with trumpeting, Swans.
Praise them with the loud
Cymbals of your honking, Canada Geese,
The flashing of your beauty, Wood Ducks,
The whirring of wings, bronzy Pheasants,
Your laughter, Loons!
Extol them with nearly two hundred
Different hosannas, Sweet Singers.

Let every Whitetail praise them,
Waving its furry flag,
Let every Beaver click its teeth,
Or jubilantly slap water with its tail.

Let everything praise the referral
Committee and the Lord
That these tens of thousands of acres
Of earth can remain a refuge —
That your flyways will not be ravaged
By any giant bird that whines and roars.

Praise the Lord in his sanctuary,
And in yours.

Obit Reread

Too strange an account to be doubted
is the way the lammergeier
bone-breaking bearded vulture
death bird with a red-rimmed eye
hung there in the sky
about to drop a land-tortoise
to crack it on rocks —

when sun caught the bald pate
of Aeschylus, turning it to a light-
colored stone, and unerringly
the poet's head caught the great
bird's plummeting meal, shelling it.

Briefly, more sadly than his others, thus
reads the last tragedy of Aeschylus.

Albrecht Dürer

Child of nature,
father of etching
and master of linear design,
court painter to Maximilian I
and man at home with many angels,
how could you declare
you didn't know what beauty was?

It was there
caught in your murals, and among
your saints. It is here in your
Hands of an Apostle, in your
five-hundred-year-old Bunch of Violets,
your Little Piece of Turf,
your Owl, and your Young Hare
with its long ears.

Beauty is every Dürer.

Thoreau Calls on Whitman

> *"Each seemed planted in fast reserves,
> surveying each other curiously — like
> two beasts, each wondering what the
> other would do, whether to snap
> or run."*
> Bronson Alcott

On the first call, Whitman was away.
On the second call, picture the usually
Affable lion in his den —
Home, perhaps, from riding an omnibus
Up and down Broadway, loving
The world of men and roaring Homer
Above the roar of the carts. . . .
See him and the woods-loving buck,
Their nostrils quivering, receiving
Impressions they did not understand.

The deer was later to praise the lion
And he, celebrator of earth,
Sun, self and all animals,
Was to claim the other his brother . . .
Yet that day the two
Could pluck from their warm hearts only
Cold compliments for each other.

Coleridge, Praise

for your footnote to The Mariner
crediting "Mr. Wordsworth"
for the pair of lines he gave you
as you two walked with Dorothy
from Nether Stowey to Dulverton,
Autumn, 1797
    What better
proof that sometimes healthy poetry
is born aloud, on the move, midwifed
by Earth herself?

Wilde in the Highest City
in the United States, 1882

In Leadville, Colorado, this April night
the wit from Ireland is lecturing on
aesthetic philosophy -- to the delight
and curiosity of rugged men.
So well is Cellini's autobiography
received, the miners ask why Wilde has not
brought the sculptor with him, and when told he
is no longer living, one asks who shot
him. Using Botticelli as another bridge
between himself and this mountainous place
wanting cultivation, poised on the edge
of bettering itself, Wilde with candor and grace
pronounces, *"Life without industry is sin,
and industry without art is barbarism."*

Standing up the Sweet Corn

Had the wind and rain not tilted stalks
at 45 degree angles, north by northeast,
we'd not have gone down the rows
acute-angled ourselves. Borers, too,
had done their share of bending corn.
Ants that found us worse than the storm,
exposing egg-sacks among grasses uprooted,
zigzagged wildly. We leaflifted
the green jewel of a chrysalis
dotted with gold that would bring forth
its monarch — floater, dancer, glider, dipper
depending on its wing-tilt.

Standing up, slanting a look to the area
of angularities where we had righted,
wronged, disturbed, composed,
committed larceny, we concluded
in his boyhood Euclid,
that sower of the seeds of geometry,
must have worked in a garden.

For "Madame Cezanne in the Conservatory"

So quietly you sit among the plants
Black-gowned, hands folded, we are curious:
What of the you behind your countenance

He painted like a mask that neither enchants
Nor repels? Still life you were to him, not us.
So quietly you sit among the plants

Who would do a hundred sittings if Cezanne's
Pleasure demanded it, the question is —
What of the you behind your countenance?

Whether he lived in Paris or Provence
Were you lonely or happy? Mysterious,
So quietly you sit among the plants.

It's certain you never dreamed his influence
Upon modernist art, his mastery, plus.
What of the you behind your countenance:

Was ever there a budding of romance
For the man at once ugly and timorous?
So quietly you sit among the plants —
What of the you behind your countenance?

What Bird?

> *"I paint as a bird sings."*
> C. Monet

What bird was he, singing those luminous
water lilies at Giverny in his pool
over and over, capturing various

changes of atmosphere and light? How tell
his species — who sang poplars, sang the Thames
in thirty-seven views and who could trill

women and children gently, chrysanthemums
in their effulgence? What bird innocent
of cages, singing his spontaneous hymns

to radiance, was this who was indifferent
to well-earned adulation? Say, what *rara
avis* was he, everlastingly intent

on surpassing strains that he had sung before?
Shelley's "blithe spirit," born to sing and soar?

2

The Game Players

Now that all three have departed (west,
or in whatever direction animals go)
remember their whimsicalities best:

how the old trotter, when you pretended
to chase him, would snort and, rolling his eyes,
race with a devil in his hooves, upended —

how the old cat at a signal would flex
his legs and streak through the rooms, turning
sassily toward you from his chair, King's X,

how the old dog would humor you, tensed jowl
for jowl, in the growling dialogs
you staged, so long as he had the last growl.

Remember the delight in them you had
for their best possible memorials.
All three were always sad to feel you sad.

Villanelle for Prairie Dogs

You who had flourishing cities of your own
Larger than London, Paris, and New York combined
Have dwindled now to an occasional town.

It's not that you're retrogressive. Rather, down
The years progressiveness has undermined
You who had flourishing cities of your own —

Till more than ninety percent of you are gone.
Once hobnobbers with buffalo, maligned,
You have dwindled now to an occasional town,

Yet remain home-lovers, winsome. Light brown
Jack-in-the-boxes expertly designed,
You who had flourishing cities of your own

Still hold your own with hawk, coyote, your known
Predators — but being powerless with our kind
Have dwindled now to an occasional town.

All we can do is give you a place in the sun
Of respect, however belatedly and confined —
You who had flourishing cities of your own
And have dwindled now to an occasional town.

Missing Red Squirrel

So *there* you are —
you hadn't gone far, but
it might as well have been Zanzibar

as to this grass
hollow: unsassy, with
no eyes left for being glassy,

no frolic in you.
How very thin you are
with no muscle now, nor sinew!

We've heard it said
you earned your red hue
carrying lightning as you sped

down through the air —
but it didn't prepare you
for being taken so unaware

by the lightning-strikes
of enemy beaks and
hollow-tree-protecting shrieks.

Couldn't you, elf,
and lightning yourself,
have outzigzagged this epitaph?

For a Lady Naming a Chipmunk "Ethelred the Unready"

It's clear *your* Ethelred's unreadiness
This morning is for taking a proffered nut
To nibble or store — a far less serious
Matter than ruling England well (without
Good 'counsel'). With his ripe-chokecherry eyes
Upon the gift, his fuzzy tail aflirt,
Only your kindly hand has given him pause,
And may for days. Yet chitteringly alert,
Astonished even, he need not contend
With Danes invading his garden, under Sweyn
Nor young Canute — need never flee for his
Life to some orchard Normandy. Your friend,
Ready at length, will scamper through his reign
Not once aware how fortunate he is.

Night Mission

> *"What do geese dream of?*
> *They dream of grain."*
> Proverb

What do foxes dream of?
They dream of geese.

What do I dream of? Wish
Fulfillment, or past delight —
But last night
I dreamed of a newly dug
Hole and a burly dog
Waiting above it.

All day I have wondered whether
A fox was down there,
Or my favorite wishes, unaware
Of a rude setback, yet scrabbling
Up the sides together.

Either way,
Being on the side of foxes,
I must return tonight
And make friends with the dog.

The Hosing Down

All of the words with which we come forearmed
To the hyena's cage: *abominable,*
Bristled and *massive,* buffalo *thigh-bone crushers,*
Carrion-eaters with *maniacal laughter,*
Cowards even, go down the drain with water
The hose ejects. The spotted pair leaps, biting
The elusive jets with jaws not made for such,
Nipping each other, racing away, returning
To attack the sparkle boisterously, much
As the pampered spaniel does in our backyard.
Dissolved for them is prison, for us a myth
Until the plaything peters out, bit to death.

Cat Fight, 5 a.m.

I know it was profane, though I have no accurate
pithy, alphabetical, phonic and precise
dictionary for profanity in *cat*.

They rolled, they screamed bloodcurdlingly, they spat
out their expletives in a way that wasn't nice.
I know it was profane, though I have no accurate

way of translating such cacophony as that
right under my window without the device
of a dictionary for profanity in *cat*.

They broke for needed breathers, but were up and at
each other's throat and belly in a trice —
which I know was profane, though I've no accurate

way to gage the bellicosity — ears all flat,
tails lashing like fat bullwhips — without a concise
dictionary for profanity in *cat*.

At ringside for fifteen rounds of feline hate
I heard the unrepeatable (my blood was ice)
and I know it was profane, though I have no accurate
dictionary for profanity in *cat*.

The Cats of Colette

Did Krô, Kapok, and Muscat
come promptly when you called them to eat?
and Touteu-Petiteu, Minionne,
Toune and Pichinette?
What of the five others — and the one
'who was called Mini-Mini because
he's got no name, poor thing'?

Sensitive, your lovelies must have been
aware that you, so sensitive, too,
studied the workings of their feline minds,
their ups and downs.

                         It seems of no
consequence that their color was
'grey, grey, grey, and grey again . . . '
Their names still paint a glorious Bow.

The White Cat

What's this: hoary barbed wire strung from tree
to tree where a clothesline hung? Gray chickenwire
now feathered out in whitest filigree?
Each weed-stalk we'd ignored an ivory spire?
The weeping willow frozen in a cascade,
even oaks alabastered? Spruces inquire
if they're not royalty, ermine-arrayed.

Speak not too loudly, lest vibrations tremble
this exquisite new world of masquerade.
The seven sparrows coming to feed resemble
closely their former selves, yet the white cat
who watches them fly up and reassemble
may well be a creature of fantasy begot
to tiptoe throught this hoarfrost habitat.

Interview with Rover's Ghost

Pope's *Bounce* and Byron's *Boatswain,*
Scott's *Maida,* Stevenson's *Wattle,*
Dickens' *Timber* and *Flush,* too,
were all illustrious. *Rover*
                what of you?
"I lived in the Hopkins house
                and yard . . . "
And so wear the borrowed aura
                of son Gerard?
"No."
What did you do, now prowling
                fame's edges?
"Well, when he was young, I bit
                Robert Bridges."

Reply to an Inquiry as to Why
I Haven't Answered a Letter

I am the cat out walking who knows
she will return for supper, yet goes
almost out of earshot — not quite.

She will come eagerly before the night
has fallen, after the call goes out,
but in her own good time, never doubt.

Last Night I Dreamed

I was a cat, my major qualification
being green-eyed (and left alone not growing
lonely nor bored). Immediate transformation

made me a pussyfooter in my glowing
sable so velvety the night winds were
as unaware of me as any mouse going

home before dawn. My enigmatic purr
was suddenly *there*, no winding up, no learning.
Wherever I went my feline savoir faire

made friends for me, though independence burning
was a fire I'd not imagined hitherto.
But the climax of my dream before returning

home was a biological breakthrough:
I knew I was fetching, *and I knew I knew.*

The Prophet

> *"What is man without the beasts? If all
> the beasts were gone, man would soon die
> from a great loneliness of spirit.
> For what-ever happens to the beasts,
> soon happens to man.
> All are connected."*
> Chief Seattle

In your mind's eye, did you see the least
Dusky Seaside Sparrow disappearing,
certain Whales as well, the Ivory-bearing Beast
threatened, not by man you knew as caring
but by the men consumed by cruel greed?

Did you, sad for lost majesty and near it
frail butterflies and birds, even as we, not plead
                                 with the Great Spirit

for some authority miraculous
to save Beasts for themselves, and oh, for us?

3

Bone to Pick with Silken Creatures

As if you murines didn't have enough
housekeeping sites in burrows, cupboards, coat
pockets that hang in closets, plus the fluff

of unused bird nests, now we find you out
in each impromptu dwelling place. What rare
mouse arrogance to set your tables d'hote

or a la carte of dog food in our air
cleaners, or decide our air conditioning
systems are comfortable for you! How dare

you enter our brake calipers, and sing
your nest-songs under dashes, even hobnob
with blowers, to your sorrow? One more thing:

so minimally seen, how is it you rob
our pockets maximally, each "mouse job"?

(A mechanic's estimate is from $28 to $150
for each repair bill.)

For a Mexican Spiny Pocket Mouse

You sounded like a mouse-sized porcupine —
Exotic certainly, before we met —
A boy might slip in his pocket now and then.

But *Loimys irroratus*, you're a "plain
Mouse sprinkled with dew," so we can well forget
You sounded like a mouse-sized porcupine.

And furthermore, the pockets are your *own*,
Fur-lined, and you're no socializing pet
A boy might slip in his pocket now and then.

When foraged seeds are emptied and you dine,
You groom your pockets, turning them inside out
Though you sounded like a mouse-sized porcupine.

What other rodent is able to combine
so charming a name and habits? Never let
A boy slip you in his pocket now and then.

A poet named you seeing you in starshine,
Evolved to the nth degree of daintiness, yet
You sounded like a mouse-sized porcupine
A boy might slip in his pocket now and then.

Mouse in the Morning

There are no marks on the cold cart, showing
how many frantic leaps you made
trying to clear its rim.

There is no way of knowing
how many hours the two-wheeled metal
thing was your Bastille-trap.

All that is known for certain is this:
that your amazing silken vibrissae,
no longer worried, are half as long as
your body, half as long as
your two-and-a-half inch tail —

and this: that you need not have died
so young and so soon
had we turned the cart in the shed
upside-down yesterday afternoon.

Horseshoe Crabs

Moonlight, high water, and they in shiny
Dark helmets emerging from the froth
Mated more safely than their nearest kin,
The spiders: females dropping clutches in
Scooped-out nests in the sand, then both
Males and females moving to other nests, their spiny
Telsons behind them.
                            But search as I may
This morning, low tide, I cannot discover
Hoofprints made by shoes without any horses
Eerily, eagerly bent upon their courses —
Left by a solitary arthropod lover.
One doubts the astonishments of night, by day.

A Snake in the Hands —

a docile bull, or an indigo
or blue racer, cool
to the touch, slipping
a clean coil on coil
through fingers at stiff attention,
flicking its tongue now
smelling and tasting,
getting to know
surfaces where its belly-plates
walk with a ripple,
slowly shedding the stigma
worn since the apple —
is worth at least a hundred and two
snakes peered at in the Zoo.

The Frog

> is "as we all know,
> a foul and filthy creature,
> abiding in foul places,
> as bogs and miry plashes...
> and at night peeping out
> with the head above the water,
> making a hateful noise
> with many others of his sort
> till the day appear again."
> Bishop Gervase Babington (1550-1610)

Begging your pardon, Bishop Babington,
what frogs could you have known, so clearly you
seemed over-intent on casting a stone?

Though you could not foresee the jumping fun
at Calaveras, you'd have damned that, too,
begging your pardon, Bishop Babington.

Even the famous frogs Aesopian,
respected, pointing morals, had little to do
with lessening your intent to cast a stone.

Why were vocal sacs ballooning 'spring has begun'
so hateful to you, so foul their rendezvous?
Begging your pardon, Bishop Babington,

after your heart must have been the prescription:
'eye of newt and toe of frog' in witches' brew —
who seemed over-intent on casting a stone.

You annoy us, offend us, pleasuring in one
talking frog among many, as we do,
and begging your pardon; Bishop Babington,
what did it profit you to cast your stone?

Rotifer, Rotifer

when my back was turned
your drop of algae-flowered
lake in the well-slide
dried—
and I thought you who this morning
were a very next-to-nothing
had died.

I mourned your microscopic
wheel turning, turning,
getting you food and getting you
about.
But now I've recreated
your green depths, animalcule,
and, wheel turning, you are off
surely with an infinitesimal
shout!

Rotifer, rotifer, you
help to reinforce, renew
my faith in living again.

4

Draw at the Zoo

The great horned owl and the red foxes here
Within one habitat, eyeing each other,
Have more in common than the space they share.

Though all are nocturnal, the yellow eyes dare
The quadrupeds daily to ruffle a feather
As the great horned owl and the red foxes here

Are stalemated hopelessly. The red pair,
Measuring the talons of their ferocious brother,
Have more in common that the space they share

With the hoo-hoo-hooer: neither can be preyer
Any more than if each were held by a tether.
While the great horned owl and the red foxes here

Seem to mark time in their dilemma, elsewhere
We in our encounters, not resolved either,
Have more in common than the space they share

With us: the wit to win, and ego to spare.
We, unlike them, will break our deadlocks whether
Or not the horned owl and the red foxes here
Have more in common than the space they share.

Take-over at the Symphony

A dissimulation of birds
Takes possession of both
Hands of the conductor, by turn —
    Woodcock plunges in its
    Courtship flight,
    Loon flaps to be air-borne,
    Hawk glides, tilting;
    Goldfinch undulates
    Sunflower to sunflower,
    Skylark spirals;
    Hummingbird hovers, darts,
    Chickadee twig-hops,
    Barn swallow free-flows;
    Crow sculls into wind,
    Shrike fiercely strikes,
    Golden eagle dives —
And presently returns them
Relaxed yet intense, delicate
Yet robust, their grace
Undiminished, to Seiji Ozawa.

Puffins

clownlets unaware,
dance on your orange-red feet
who dance only in courtship,
waddle on your toes
with your comical gait,
clack your red, yellow, and black bills
for you are no songsters.

Celebrate this:
the first puffin hatched
on Eastern Egg Rock off Maine
to *return*
after more than a century
has gently landed!

Celebrate calling the windswept
island home again,
while we celebrate you
jesters, perhaps, with bills
puffed out to carry several fish
at the same time — but no fools.

Filling the Suet Basket

If the beast who gave up this bounty
could return and see, between two blinks
of those late liquid eyes, chickadee,
downy, nuthatch, jay and starling
taking pillows of energy and warmth
against the harshnesses of night,
it would not recognize its own.
Nor would a beak-prick of this hard
crumbly fat that cradled the beast's
kidneys and loins be felt...

Yet even a goose, intelligent,
would never detect its down that pads
your jacket. And you yourself
have likely forgotton words you plucked
from around your heart: *"The strong go on"*
that cushion me still
against adversity.

"Crows in the Wheat Fields"
(painted the year he took his life)

I have counted forty-four crows
Swooping over those Auvers fields of wheat,
        Darkening the sky

Already menacing, and pulling
The horizon to us and Vincent Van Gogh.
        The work, with little

To focus on, is one 'of sadness
And extreme solitude,' he admitted.
        But look back to that

Summer of 1890: picture
His shot frightening crows, opening vistas.
        See the dead-end road

In the rough fields miraculously
Extending to point his tormented being
        To peace at last.

Macaw at the Zoo

We salute this gold and blue pennant
tapering to its long pointy tail.
(We give its beak a wide berth, though.)
Darwin thought the macaws' taste of blue
and yellow 'inharmonious,' and wondered
at the bad taste of their screams as well.
Our words are 'magnificent,' 'fortunate' aware
that smugglers have reduced the kin
left in the world to *rare*.

How different when Columbus sighted large
flocks of macaws streaming southwesterly.
Not knowing Florida lay straight ahead,
the navigator veered to follow the birds —
arriving at San Salvadore, and changing
the course of Spanish exploration.

"Never did the flight of birds,"
wrote Baron Alexander von Humbolt,
"have more important consequences."

Conversely, man has ever had important
impact upon the flight of birds.

Courtship Dance
of the Common House Sparrow

Shades of the intricate courtship patterns
of African weaver birds, partridge dances,
the water ballet of grebes, the "dancing-party"
of birds-of-paradise in a tree!

You, the "uncomfortably familiar and
vulgarly lively" bird of **Buffon**,
now suddenly jig, bow, bounce, wings
drooping, tail spreading unvulgarly —
then fling yourself up in a circle around
your female. Now you perform a peasant
dance, displaying black bib and white cheeks
to advantage. *Lovely.*

And I had thought you mounted with neither
pattern nor preliminary, weaver bird yourself.
Where were my eyes?
What have I missed of other fleeting
preludes, introductions, entreaties
               for success in love?

May Morning on the Game Farm

Caretakers are gathering Trumpeter Swans,
white, white, a few protesting noisily.
It is made easier by clipping the wings
of this once-threatened species.

        Have the two men
working matter-of-factly, yet admiringly,
heard Robinson Jeffers' plea to love wildness,
        specifically the wild swan?

Thirty-two of the great birds will be flown
to Tamarac Reserve in northwestern Minnesota
in Air National Guard Planes — an affront
to wings needing to thunder again
in their own right.

See the caretakers collecting and casually
deglorifying Trumpeters.

5

Talking to the Swans

In her wrinkled raincoat, babushka, galoshes
The old woman comes to the pond, bearing seeds.
Once we inquired, "Were you talking to the geese?"
           "No — I was talking to the swans."

If she found a unicorn sporting with antelope
It would prance up to her, eat from her hand,
And she would tell anyone matter-of-factly,
           "I was communing with a unicorn."

Moving among angels, she would find archangels.
Yet why am I struck by her being eclectic?
From the ordinary, the common run,
The prevalent, middle-of-the-road, so-so,
The inarticulate, colorless, the obscure,
Even truly interesting, honest, good men,
           Didn't I select you?

Bow Tie

Last night your bow tie was pressed
By the chin-rest of the violin
Of the artist from Uruguay
Throughout the Vieuxtemps Concerto.

Loaned to him, the satin of the folds
Absorbed the brilliant cadenzas bowed
By this man discovered as a boy
By Fritz Kreisler . . .

This morning I sense the tie changed.

As the folds of draperies at the Met
Must have caught and held rare vibrations
When Caruso made his New York debut
As the duke in "Rigoletto". . .

As the cobbled streets of Rome
Must have taken thunder to their centers
When Caesar in triumph thundered home . . .

Your tie in its minuscule way
Shivers in ecstasy.

Tardy Thanksgiving

What a number of things
There are to be grateful to:
The enraged bull (not of rings

And *Oles,* but the corral)
that released you in time;
The lake bottom, impersonal

And oozy, that caught you, diving,
but let you work free and surface;
The torpedoes arriving

A moment too late to gut
Your ship; other accidents,
Great and small, failing to shut

Off the bright circuits of blood and air
Making you you — and those two:
Your mother and father. Rare

You'd be for such reasons alone
And to be cherished. Yet I
First loved you, not having known.

Cycles

That morning on the Galapagos
When Roger Tory Peterson received a haircut
from a friend, a Darwin finch gathered
the silken locks to line its nest.
Amazing, we agree, how the little bird
brought the studies of the two illustrious men
full circle there after more than a century.

Why are we less astonished at larger
and smaller cycles: Halley's Comet returning,
the year from one vernal equinox to the next,
cicada nymphs emerging from earth-beds
after seventeen years, becoming ruby-eyed,
lemmings advancing stolidly to the sea
every so often?

And let's wonder at our own full circle:
my admiring you from a distance
and after two decades — and your ship
in the Merchant Marine just missed
by torpedoes, our private metamorphoses,
light that shone steadily for each of us
yet tailed away — you stood at my door
one April noon, smiling, and came in . . .

Request

Let us respect all forests in each other —
Thus being some wiser than good King Solomon
Who sent "fourscore thousand hewers" to the hills
To cut the glorious cedars of Lebanon.

Lest we create erosion in each other,
Or at best grasses, and thorny thickets' onslaught,
Fell not the sloping woodlands of my musing.
I shall not harm the high timber of your thought.

Moot Point

Bringing you a handful of raspberries clinging
redly to their bushes in the morning mist
I've asked myself it they were worth the bringing.

It's someone else's thicket with a catbird singing
incomparably from which I couldn't resist
bringing you a handful of raspberries. Clinging

to the rest, I dropped two spheres belonging
to you on the kitchen floor. Both were promptly lost.
I've asked myself if they were worth the bringing

since searching on the red inlaid I went banging
down upon them suddenly, injuring my wrist.
Bringing you a handful of raspberries clinging

to their bush resulted in a ticket and haranguing
on our way to the Clinic, for a red light missed.
I've asked myself if they were worth the bringing

though I wanted to share the day's early ringing
out of sweet song and bounty. Yet why do I persist,
after bringing you a handful of raspberries stinging
us, in asking myself if they were worth the bringing?

6

Poem to the Brain

Dear wrinkled mass inside my cranium,
ten-billion nerve celled, 1500-gram
weight probably, but infinitely more —
why haven't I sat down to write before?

How tolerant you are, uncelebrated,
to keep me seeing, hearing, animated,
thinking (or choosing not to), loving, too,
and praising less deserving ones than you.

Now we are mindful, Brain, that you are cleft
into your hemispheres of Right and Left:
your imagistic side, and logical . . .
and you are impressive in duality.
But be the familiar you have been to me,
dear gelatinous lump inside my skull.

Song for Red Blood Cells

Your birth in my marrow is a secret doing:
not even announced, as is the latest litter
the neighbor's cat is proud of, blind and mewing;
nor once observed, like spiderlings, to better
advantage moving in sun; and scarcely thought
about from cut to cut, till some red-letter
day in surgery. Your growing up to float
constantly, busily bearing oxygen
upon the Plasma, each in your red boat,
to nourish me again, again, again
has seldom been acknowledged, never cheered.
Yet you who sing in me shall have your own
poems to celebrate you, here's my word —
and you will sing the better for having heard.

On Discovering that One of My Three Brains is Reptilian

There are times I use my oldest brain
                almost exclusively:
sunning, swimming, finding food, shelter,
                fighting or fleeing.

Knowing that I share an ancient gift
                with mud turtle,
basilisk, alligator, anaconda takes
                getting used to, humbles me.

Yet I am glad that it lies there,
                surrounded
by my old and new mammalian brains.
It keeps my feet on the ground.

Talking to My Cells

Nothing formal, I promise them. The very
Thought of recognizing title, category,
Composition, function, even status
                After mitosis
Can tie my tongue in disconcerting fright.
No pep talk either, I tell them, which they greet
Curiously with renewed vigor, and
                No ax to grind.

Somehow it never ceases to amaze
My cells that I've no plan to criticize them,
Speaking to them on our intercom.
                Just praising them
For holding my whole world inside my skin
Together, and for being skin, not too thin --
And thanking them for being teachable
                And resourceful
Can set them humming with cellular good cheer.
All I can think of is the way my ear
In childhood, pressed to a telephone pole, heard
                Such singing there!

Oh, to Wear the Bones of a Bird Inside

of me, delicate, many containing air
cavities for unlimited flight, I said—
Or, leather-soled and heeled by day, to wear
the velvet-falling pads of Felidae,
or to speak like a susurrent stream to her familiars.

                        True, *my* bones liberally supply
red blood cells from their miracle of marrow,
and when have I celebrated them? When have I
said, "Feet, you bear me on the strict and narrow
and even when I stray"? Or paused to be
grateful my voice is gentle, although arrow-
sharpness may fly out now and then?

to wear the bones of a bird inside of me . . .

7

Post Card from Norway

When you wrote from Bergen,
    mornings there had been
"spring-like and blissful, fresh with many flowers"
(for us to read upon a day when ours
was summer-rain logged) and you added when
the space was nearly filled, that you had seen
the Edvard Grieg home in its sunlit wood —
did you imagine that his "Morning Mood"
would presently drift about us, golden-green,
enchanting phrase by phrase and bird by bird,
till your familiar writing all but blurred?
Did you suspect for a moment, when you sent
your scenic post card via northern air,
reporting to us how you were and where,
you would charm our day's remainder with Peer Gynt?

A Matter of Nomenclature

Three hundred harpists gather from around
the world, commemorating Henriette
Renie's 100th birthday*, and the papers
call it a 'conference'? Why not
a magnificent 'melody of harpists'?

Think of the concentration of vibrations,
the power of harmony if all
the drifting arpeggios in Ravel's
and Debussy's music were caught
by three hundred harps.

Even the gods entering Valhalla
had only six sets of fingers dancing divinely
over harp-strings, at Wagner's command.

'Conference' is hardly the word for a host
of artists sitting gracefully holding
their fiendishly hard-to-play instruments —
and playing heaven down.

* 1975

At the Concert

Carmen Cavallaro Plays Eddie Duchin

Before the Poet of the Piano could outpour
Eddie Duchin he realized poems by *him*
were more than a matter of image and metaphor,
of content and rhythm and musical rhyme scheme.
Creating the poems called for the nth degree
of inspiration and expression.
                    At length acclaim
followed his brilliant Duchin poetry,
and only one questions haunts.
                    When Eddie sat
down in New York to play for afternoon tea
dances, some ladies at the exquisite
interpretation of a song they adored
wept softly, unashamedly over it.

Does anyone weep here, over Duchin heard
from the celebrated Poet of the Keyboard?

8

Old Photo of a Young Teacher

Here you are without your brood
of fifty pupils. I picture you
always in control of a room,
standing tall, your eyes intently
taking charge, saving your clear voice
for reading aloud, for drawing out
inquiring minds; for holding spell-downs,
teaching arithmetic: 1+1 to square root.

I see you best as grammarian,
coaching your own child later till at four
he disconcertingly corrected others.

The striking you took part in was to light
matches to kindling, though salaries
were preposterously low, hours long...
Illness pursued you later. Yet here you are,
Mother, in bloom, perennially young.

Mother as Student of Physiology

In your high school notebook the nervous systems
you diagramed are never on edge, and surely
the hardy four-chambered muscle you pictured
here on page seven seems ready to pump forever.

The skeletons you drew could frighten one, nights,
the vertical section of an eye read thoughts,
the taste buds distinguish the salt of a hand
turning the pages.

Yet, despite excellent marks, you didn't learn
the inestimable value of calmness.
No one taught you how to keep the nucleated
red cells from reducing themselves to anemia.
Sketching a perfect heart, you couldn't have known
your three-dimensional one was to lag, later,
pick itself up with primings and our need
of its effusing love, then stop too soon.

Amaryllis Unfolding

More amazing than your cerise
whispering, your sudden shouting,
glad of ultimate release
from sepals, though never doubting,

is the way your silks — like a man's
breast-pocket handkerchief, like laces
in a bride's trousseau, or a fan's
glory, when opened, graces

its user, Giant Lily — is how,
folded with extraordinary care
by the flower-Maker, your petals
unperturbedly waited there
till now.

Father and the Blue Shirt

Impulsively I touched the crispy
sleeve of a shirt on a rack — and reached
across decades to touch your arm.
This chambray was heavier than the shirts
you wore, which were faded except for streaks
your suspenders criss-crossed in back.

I saw you coming in from garden work,
your blue shirt sweaty, bringing
radishes and lettuce crisp even in sun.
I saw you returning from fishing,
your shirt mussed under a jacket,
happily bearing sunnies. I watched you,
stooping a little, balancing Goldy
the tomcat between your rounding shoulders.

And suddenly I missed you more
than I had since you left those untroubled
uncomplicated blue chambray summers.

Father Recalled as Dinner Companion

Now I discover, half a life from *then*,
How you, a non-worrier, once wept about
My eating too little, my being too thin.

Convincingly I could have pointed out
I lived in a house of small bones, with high
Metabolism; dreaded being stout.

I daren't have said your silences were wry
Bread I could seldom break; your gruffness would
Drain flavor to flatness; leave me humble pie.

I should have relished any platter of good
Dialogue on its nourishing pilau —
While I might have grown curvaceous, even, could

Laughter have been our appetizer. How
Savable seem all our lost meals, now.

Peonies

When I was no taller than the giant
peony blossoms in our yard
my parents cherished us, but spoke
to me only, never having heard
peonies grow their best when talked to.
Admirers never seemed to mention,
either, how sensitive the plants are,
requiring much appreciation.
No one informed them peony roots
tied around necks were "remedie
against the falling sickness." And what's
more: fifteen seeds in wine were
a cure for the night Mare . . .

Unaware that Apollo used this flower
bursting from its ant-opened bud
to heal the injuries of the gods —
my parents merely loved their peonies
into burning bushes every year.

9

The Lost Worm

Worse than finding a green-gorged cutworm
that has sheared a young cabbage plant
is promptly losing it near tomato vines.

Searching on hands and knees for the pudgy
offender, I think of Rousseau
studying botany on the Isle of St. Peter,
and wish for his magnifying glass.
                    I consider, too,
marking off the garden into little squares.

I remember Fabre's way of scrutinizing
his plot of ground in southern France
and try this, to no avail.

My lost worm will become its predestined
owlet moth, whereupon more eggs
will hatch more larvae next year.
But the *losing* of cutworms stops here.

Error

In our hurry to aerosol-bomb the aphids
Infesting the young willow (she was weeping)
We inadvertently slayed the aphis lions
Crouching there, with tufted manes, and keeping
Their share of the green enemy at bay.
Failing to roar, they were unidentified —
But we should have suspected, in all that horde,
There would be *some* that were on our side.

Mourning Cloak

> *"I do not know whether I was then a man*
> *dreaming I was a butterfly,*
> *or whether I am now a butterfly*
> *dreaming I am a man."*
> Chuang Tzu

If being a butterfly is a matter of dreaming —
    I dream of being
Trauermantel, the 'mourning cloak,' Camberwell Beauty,
    which has little to do
with mourning, much with beauty: blue-spotted purple-brown,
    bordered with soft yellow.
Donning a slim abdomen, thorax and head needn't be difficult,
    walking with six legs might.
I can master using the watch-spring proboscis
    sucking nectar and maple sap —
while, for one earth-bound, soaring on one's own wings
    can be the dream of dreams.

And this is the *Freude* of being a mourning cloak:
    to hibernate
under a stump, rather than take a monarch's long
    wing-tattering trip,
face others' death by frost....
    How exciting to slip
out of my bed at the earliest vernal beckon —
    the *first* butterfly aloft!

Ant, Grooming

Your antennae require more care
than ours — which we attach to the roof
for black-and-white or colored reception
and leave there.

You tidily pull each feeler
through the little brush on your leg
then draw the brush through your mouth
to clean *it*. How many times a day?

But it pays off, Ant:
your reception has to be better than ours,
and the chances are that your programs
are excellent.

10

Pteranodon

The old saw that only a mother could love
you is suspect as we study you. *Could* she?
With your backward projection of bone above
your huge toothless beak, were fish your mainstay?
With your wings of skin from hindlimbs stretching
to your forelimbs — at your maturity
for a space of twenty-five feet — your hatching
must have been noteworthy if reptiles then
were oviparous . . . One artist drew you, sketching
in unkempt hairiness.
                Yet, Pteranodon,
you might have fared considerably worse.
You were no weak-winged dragon, albeit gone
by the end of the Mesozoic, and of course
could have held your own against *any* St. George
              and his horse.

Seismosaurus

*(one of the longest dinosaurs
ever discovered, 1986, New Mexico)*

Imagine, in the disproportionately small
body of *Seismosaurus*, a heart
that pumped blood up its fabulously tall
neck to its brain — and was able to impart
blood as well to its elongated tail!
Imagine leathern lungs proving adequate
for the creature to inhale deeply, exhale!

Then, when *Seismosaurus* would agitate
the earth by walking riverward, and bend
down to unclouded water to slake its thirst,
imagine lesser beings fearing the worst —
certain it was their prehistoric end!

Newcomer

The youngest of the *sauruses*, you put
no fear in me, or am I growing braver
who trembled at the thought of one huge foot
of *Seismosaurus* shaking earth? I savor
your elegance by comparison with each
crude prehistoric creature, and I reach
gladly to seek and find in you a more
apt word, *Thesaurus*, than I had used before.

11

Scenes from an Exercise

The lake was much as he remembered it
from last week: yellow-headed blackbirds
blossoming on rushes, *kricking,*
and yellow-stamened water-lilies preening.
Mallards paddled to his left,
and straight ahead the shore
was at peace with the sky.

A dragonfly ferried on his arm
while a loon, watching him, submerged
leaving no ripples, only to reappear
farther away, laughing . . .

He was unaware of time —
and his wife called him twice
for dinner before he opened his eyes
in the next room, stepped off
his deluxe rower with its adjustable
hydraulic tension, its smooth flow,
and out of his dream.

Waiting for Venus

> *A railway conductor kept his engineer*
> *waiting (12 minutes) on a sidetrack*
> *to allow Venus to pass.*
> Engineers' Journal, 1880

With far-off headlight blazing, the Sublime
One, traveling at her known velocity
of twenty-two miles/second, appeared to be
approaching. Give her room! The lost time
were vastly preferable to colliding . . .

Yet the Evening Star, millions of miles distant
speeding on her private schedule, insistent
                Failed to streak by the siding.

On Finding a Child's Dump Truck on the Road to the Dump

Battered, orange as the coach of Cinderella,
obviously you were on your last
trip — abandoned by some jaded fellow,

once transported, transporting sand in you. Outcast
of playtime, childhood even, you've a brief
reprieve here, but for you a little fast

and heavy the traffic. Oh, you'll come to grief
eventually as all things coming over
this road to limbo do, yet you'll be safe

a while now hidden in the roadside clover.
Be the spirit of possessions we have kissed
goodby, relinquished, desired to recover

but could not. Be the other good we've thrust
aside deliberately, and most missed.

Elegy

Here are more answers in your obit than we
had questions for in your geometry
classes. We considered your name: A. V.
Overn perfect for your subject, writing it
secretly $\frac{AV}{N}$.

       Alfred seems not to fit
our formal teacher, and Victor is a bit
sportslike (although you did play tennis well).
Your true age stuns us — unbelievable
that wearing your dignity and somewhat dull
gray suit you were so young, and hadn't known
more fun than visiting Yellowstone
with sister Olga, feeding bears.

       Now we've grown
too far from you and theorems we pursued
to postulate what more felicity you'd
desire than bears in some Elysian wood.

Self-Service

"No, thank you," I answered the telephone voice
asking to sell me a book on house plants
and their problems. "We have many plants
but no Problems." Actually, I meant
>no mealy bugs, mites,
>aphids, whiteflies,
>leaf-drop, droopiness,
>premature death . . . .

I didn't say our precious avocado
is about to thrust through the ceiling;
that our praying hands plant now has taken
to folding its leaves at dawn instead of dusk.
>I didn't mention non-
>praying philodendron
>is passionately in love
>with snake plant.

It certainly is no one else's affair
that the tub of spring-o'-rye winces
when the cat nibbles it for indigestion,
nor that peperomia strongly protests
               becoming a salad.
               The calendar of Easter
               cactus is faulty.
               Fuchsia is moody.

Cobra lily threateningly displays
its hood when we have shorted it on food.
All prefer rain water to slake thirst —
yet these private matters are never divulged
               to inquirers.
               In our tightly-grown
               green community
               we write our own book.

People Are Getting into Plants These Days

entering by imaginary doors in the stems,
flowing upward, studying cell structure,
feeling accepted, each being one
with his host as nearly as possible,
thinking himself a pioneer.
Yet young shoemaker Jakob Boehme,
mystic in 16th century Germany,
willed himself into a plant until
he "rejoiced with a joyously growing leaf."

Now I am searching for the right plant.
I have energy it will welcome,
secrets to tell it, much to share.
The plant can teach me supersensitivity.

Imagining myself no larger than a weevil
or corn-borer, surely I can squeeze in . . .
Leaving, however, I must become
a non-vegetarian.

Timberdoodle

Though his appearance invites ridicule
and he may well be netted if unwary,
the timberdoodle is nobody's fool.

He wears his eyes high, his long bill is a tool
probing for worms he finds so necessary
while his appearance invites ridicule.

Starting his courtship sky-dance in the cool
of dawn or evening, seemingly solitary,
the timberdoodle is nobody's fool;

up, up he spirals, using love for fuel,
wings buzzing. Then trilling like a wild canary
(though his appearance invites ridicule)

he flutters down beside a female who'll
play difficult to win, or agree to marry.
The timberdoodle is nobody's fool —

daring to give expression to his dual
woodcockian self: bogsucker, with repertory.
Though his appearance invites ridicule
the timberdoodle is nobody's fool.

Incident at Camp

Remember when we went riding at Jenny Lake
in Jackson Hole, Wyoming? I chose the small
docile paint. You said you would take
the heavy white horse.

>Just then as a tall
>bay drew alongside us
>the young man astride it
>paused to ejaculate
>bitterly, *"I hate horses!"*
>   Lest he activate

our two, we promptly rode off...

I looked back and it was clear
the rider himself was rampantly
Fear-ridden.

Snow-Cave

Stepping out last midnight to distribute
early-bird breakfasts, you likely wouldn't know
for certain the indefinable scent
teasing your nostrils was the smell of snow.

You would need to have dug laboriously
with a child's shovel in a hard-packed drift,
preferably alone, until you had a cave.
Kneeling in it you would need to have sniffed

happily walls and security commingled
much as loving in your real house — unaware
in your naivete snow-caves fall in,
love may fall out for any reason, anywhere.

Muse Away

Suspecting you are unavoidably detained,
I have searched for you in inscrutable
blue eyes of my cat, in the water-filled
trumpets of a pitcher plant, in a spider's
tunnel, thinking her trap-door may have slammed
shut on unfortunate you. I have stood below
an owl's cavity nest, looked into ant-lions' pits.

Could you be wedged inside a bulging pocket
our chipmunk-in-residence wears inside his cheek,
or worse, interred by a pair of sexton beetles?
Or, perish the thought! did you metamorphose
into a clone of **Kafka**'s giant cockroach?
Even so, you are far more welcome back
than you might suppose.

Note to be Taped to A Door-Knocker

The news is so disturbing I am off
for a cruise on Mare Serenitatus,
and after that its nearby sister Mare
Tranquilitatus — avoiding Crisium,
and troubled Oceanus Procellarum,
and Mare Frigoris.
                        I may be detained
by Lacus Somniorum, dreamer of dreams
that I am, and pause to pay my deep respects
to Craters of Archimedes and of that
stargazer, thinker, Copernicus. Don't look
for my return until the news is better,
or I cannot remain away from Earth.